Self-Esteem and Your Inner Child

GLENYS YAFFE

Copyright © 2015 Glenys Yaffe

All rights reserved. No part of this book may be reproduced or transmitted in any form or by any means, electronic or mechanical, including photocopying, recording or by any information storage and retrieval system, without prior permission in writing from the author.

Cover Design by BookPOD
Printed and bound in Australia by BookPOD

Cover Design by BookPOD
Printed and bound in Australia by BookPOD

A Cataloguing-in-Publication entry is available from the National Library of Australia

ISBN: 978-1-925457-02-5 (pbk.)
eISBN: 978-1-925457-03-2

CONTENTS

Preface		vii
Chapter 1	Where Does It All Begin? Developmental Patterns	1
Chapter 2	The Inner Child	7
Chapter 3	How Do We Go About Changing?	21
Chapter 4	Idealised Images	35
Chapter 5	Getting In Our Own Way	41
Chapter 6	Projections	47
Chapter 7	Core Issues	51
Chapter 8	Compromising and Adapting to Our Core Issues	63
Chapter 9	Relationships and Self-Esteem	73
Chapter 10	What Now?	85
Bibliography		90

Acknowledgements

Thank you to my family and friends for their support and feedback through the many months of writing this book, and for their encouragement during my writer's blocks and times of doubt. Also for their patience during my vacillation between frustration and excitement.

Thank you to my Writers' Group at Phoenix Park, who have always been there as constructive and valued critics, and particularly to Nicole Hayes, our leader and teacher, who has consistently provided wonderful learning opportunities and encouragement throughout the process of making sense of my thoughts and creativity.

And thank-you also to my clients, who have enhanced my forever ongoing learning, and for the privilege of allowing me into their world as they have engaged in the process of their own "re-parenting".

Preface

In my twenty-seven years as a psychologist and psychotherapist, people have come to see me for a wide range of issues. What I have discovered is that whatever the presenting problem might be, people frequently also have a low level of self-esteem. Sometimes they are painfully conscious of this; at other times it hovers below the surface, unrecognised or hidden from awareness, perhaps covered over by external measures of success or achievement.

Unfortunately, for as long as we don't feel a real sense of our intrinsic worth, we don't enjoy life's full potential; we're busily trying to find means to compensate for our lack of belief that we're inherently okay.

This book helps identify the elements that get in the way of a fulfilling sense of "I'm okay in the world", and provides tools to assist in the emergence of a stronger sense of self. It provides a way of reframing our negative self-talk. The framework used is an effective tool for achieving this goal, and does much more than a more cognitive approach, since it includes not only a logical way of turning around the negative messages that have become habitual, but also incorporates the childhood issues that continue to influence our adult relationship with ourselves and others.

Chapter One

WHERE DOES IT ALL BEGIN? DEVELOPMENTAL PATTERNS

It is helpful, in trying to understand how we come to be as we are, to reflect back to the beginning: the environment we grew up in.

American psychologist Erik Erikson devised a model that is useful for our purposes here. He believed that a combination of biological, psychological and cultural influences in our early years interact to shape the way we develop into adults. Erikson conceptualised life development in terms of eight stages, five childhood stages and three adult stages. The five stages of childhood, defined by Erikson, were also adopted by John Bradshaw, in his book *Homecoming*.

These five child stages[1]: infancy, toddler, pre-school, school-age and adolescence, each contain specific, normal dependency needs. How well these needs are met determines how we emerge from childhood, with each stage having a potentially positive or negative psychological outcome. So if there has been what Donald Winnicott called "good enough mothering", (or good enough parenting), the primitive, totally dependent infant has a good emotional grounding. To the degree our needs are fulfilled, we grow up with a healthy self-esteem at our centre, a sense that we're essentially acceptable and lovable. Failure to receive what we need, cumulative through each stage, means that our foundations are more shaky. So we carry a wound: at our centre, rather than self-esteem, we have a basic anxiety. In psychotherapist and author Karen Horney's words, we carry a fear of being "isolated and helpless in a potentially hostile world". Although we may not be conscious of this anxiety, from a very early stage of life we nevertheless develop patterns to protect us from experiencing the inner discomfort. These patterns are adaptive at such an early stage of life, since they help us to survive emotionally. At this tender age we've not yet developed the psycho-emotional tools to deal with our inner fears.

The patterns are like masks we wear, and may take many shapes; these might, for example, include

- The good girl or good boy (the people-pleaser)
- The rebel
- The over-achiever
- The under-achiever
- The helper/saviour/fixer
- The avoider

and many more.

The unfortunate consequences of these originally helpful patterns is that we start to identify with our masks, and believe this is who we really are; our *real self* becomes obscured behind our masks, which come to form our persona, or *false self*.

The patterns that were adaptive when we were little become maladaptive as we transport them into our adult life. For instance, the good girl/boy part of us that persists into our adult years might lead us to attend only to what others want of us, or what we think they want of us. We've developed the habit of being "people-pleasers". But in doing this we tend to negate ourselves and our *own* needs, for fear that otherwise others will not love or accept us unless we serve *their* needs.

This is a huge price to pay for safety. And for as long as we hold onto our masks, our defences against pain, we're distancing ourselves from a connection with our real selves. In distancing ourselves in this way we're not honouring and accepting who we really are. We've come to believe that we're not inherently lovable, but that we have to *be* the persona we've developed in order to be okay.

The good news is that it is possible to gradually learn that whilst we needed this protection when we were at an immature stage of life, as adults we've the strength and ability to deal with the residues of our past, let go of our old patterns, feel a stronger sense of self and live a richer life.

Moreover, we can learn ways *to give ourselves* what we missed out on in our childhood. This process is sometimes known as *re-parenting*. The method I have used to help people in this process is a powerful metaphor, encompassing a concept call the *Inner Child*. This is a means of describing the range of childhood patterns, needs, delights and discomforts that have been carried forward and are still felt by us, though not necessarily within our conscious awareness, as we live our adult lives. The framework I use is strongly influenced by the work of John Bradshaw (*Homecoming*) and Lucia Capacchione (*Recovery of Your Inner Child*).

By working with our Inner Child we can engage in our own re-parenting, and gradually shift from an inner process of self-protection from our basic anxiety to a more solid sense of self and a healthier self-esteem.

~~

(1) Erikson's Childhood Developmental Stages (with approximate ages):
    I. **Infancy**: Birth to 18 months. The important needs during infancy are parents' positive and loving care, which needs to be consistent, predictable and reliable. In particular eye contact and touch are important. If these conditions are available to us, it allows us to develop a sense of **trust**. If we don't receive enough of these conditions we're more inclined to feel a basic

II.   **mistrust** (about ourselves, others and our world) in our ensuing years.

II.   **Early childhood or Toddler stage**: 18 months to three years. During this stage we learn to master skills, as we begin to learn to walk, talk, feed ourselves and engage in toilet training. We are beginning to learn about our environment. Parents, who are our most important influence during this vulnerable stage, are often challenged by the stage of the "terrible twos", where little children are inclined to push back and say 'no', or question things in their emerging exploration of the world. Effective parenting here enhances our emerging sense of feeling capable, which augers well for us in developing a sense of **autonomy**. Whilst parents need to protect us from danger in our emerging exploration, we also need to be encouraged in our development of self-sufficiency, without fear of ridicule or criticism of our failures. Parental lack in regards to our toddler stage can propel us into a more of a subsequent sense of **shame or doubt**.

III.   **Play age (pre-school):** Three to five years. The family is important during this phase of social role identification, during which we are learning to master the world around us. At pre-school stage we copy our parents, create play situations and mimic parental roles, sometimes playing with dolls, toy phones or toy cars. We start to become more assertive. It is during this stage where, given the right circumstance, **initiative** can emerge. If the natural developmental needs are thwarted, however, **guilt** is likely to characterise our development.

IV.   **School age:** Six to twelve years. Although family is still important, the sphere of experience now extends outside the home, and school, teachers and peers now become powerful influences. During this social phase we can develop new skills and knowledge, and can develop a sense of **competence.** But if we experience feelings of inadequacy and **inferiority** with our peers, this can have a lasting impact on us.

V.   **Adolescence:** Teenage years. During this complex phase, during which we're neither child nor adult, we're involved in **identity formation,** where we're separating from family and identifying with the wider community, particularly peers, and starting to learn about the roles we'll occupy as adults. Experimentation, self-consciousness, self-absorption and confusion are not uncommon characteristics of this phase, as we struggle with the in-between stage of development. If we don't negotiate this phase effectively, this can result in **role confusion.**

Chapter Two
THE INNER CHILD

The residues of childhood remain alive within us. These include the early (often unrecognised) emotional wounds that have impacted on us, and that we carry into our adult life, characterised by the masks and patterns that were put in place to protect our emotional survival when we were young. We've seen how we needed these patterns in order to be able to get on with our young lives, because at that tender stage of development we didn't yet have the psychological infrastructure to be able to manage the emotional difficulties we were bumping into. Our psychic energy was then habitually focused on upholding these patterns as a means of avoiding the pain of our basic anxiety.

But our aim is, through *re-parenting*, to gradually be able to recognise and let go of these habits, to strengthen our boundaries, to develop more of a sense of self that embodies an acceptance of our intrinsic worth, and so experience more self-esteem. It is a gradual shift from our foundations of basic anxiety to a healed and stronger sense that we're essentially okay, with our individual mixture of strengths and limitations.

~~

Alongside the wounded remnants of our early years, there are other aspects of childhood that emotionally still dwell within us. Some parts are more obvious than others. Some have been dampened down or banished as we've been caught up in self-preservation and protecting ourselves from anxiety. For a more fulfilling way of being in the world it is helpful to recognise and integrate these vital aspects of the real self. These include:

- The Vulnerable Inner Child
- The Angry Inner Child
- The Creative Inner Child
- The Playful Inner Child
- The Spiritual Inner Child.

The Vulnerable Inner Child

This part of us includes our hurt, fear, anxiety, disappointment, loneliness and sadness. Sometimes it is a part we don't wish to acknowledge or feel. We may see it as weak. To escape the discomfort, we may deny its existence, or banish it. Our Vulnerable Child needs to feel safe to come out of hiding, which means that in the first instance it needs to be attended to and accepted by *us*.

Our vulnerable feelings are a valuable part of our psyche. It is our own vulnerability that allows us to recognise and tolerate these feelings in others. It provides us with our capacity for empathy. If we cannot tolerate our own vulnerability, it is difficult for us to see and accept these feelings in others. And most importantly, it is part of being human. We are all vulnerable beings.

Understandably, people often don't like to experience some of the feelings associated with vulnerability. People sometimes ask me, 'What's the point of feeling upset? What's the point of crying?' Apart from the reasons already mentioned above, these emotions are also often an important aspect of our healing, a healing that enables us to move on in a richer way, and to make contact with more of our real self. I remember many years ago in my own process of accepting more of my Vulnerable Inner Child, when I was going through a painful time, saying to my therapist, 'I never knew it could feel so good to feel so bad.' When we shut down feeling, we also flatten our real self, and tend to feel a numbness, or a deadness that drains our vitality. Moreover, if we close the door on our vulnerability, the door is also shut to our feelings of joy.

The Angry Inner Child

People are sometimes wary of this aspect of their inner world. This might be because of a failure to discriminate between the *feeling* of anger, and the *expression* of that emotion.

This might be particularly relevant if our only earlier exposure to anger has been through violence or abuse (which are never appropriate). Our picture of anger might then be coloured by the extreme versions we were exposed to. Physical or emotional violent expression of anger can affect our view of the emotion. If we believe the only way to *express* anger is through these destructive modes we might then try to deny the *feeling* itself. It is okay and sometimes appropriate to have an angry response, but we can find effective and constructive ways of expressing what we're experiencing.

Another reason for being wary of anger is if we've grown up as a *good girl* or a *good boy* (our "mask") anger might not then fit with our picture of how we think we "should" be responding. But there is nothing inherently wrong with feeling anger.

It may be that we need to give ourselves permission to feel what we're feeling and to explore and select from the "tool kit" of anger (i.e. the wide range of modes of expression that are available to us) for effective and non-destructive ways of dealing with the emotion. For example, this might sometimes be smashing a tennis ball across the net; or working out at the gym, (no-one gets hurt if we hit the punching bag, but it does help release some of those feelings!); for some people journaling is cathartic; or talking to a therapist and releasing through verbal expression to someone else; or learning to say to someone, 'I feel angry when you do that'.

We don't need a cannon to get rid of the ants in our kitchen, and a pea-rifle will not quite do it if we have a stampeding rhinoceros heading in our direction.

Selecting the appropriate tool can help us assert and empower ourselves without destructive aggression. It's not the *feeling* that is problematic, but rather the *inappropriate expression* of the anger, or a *disowning* of the feeling. In fact, repressed anger is often more destructive than anger that finds a healthy outlet. Its distortions are fraught with difficulties, and can erode our meaningful relationships more than when the emotion is out in the open and expressed in a constructive way. The elephant in the room will not just go away. We need to be able to give healthy expression to valid feelings of anger, or sometimes to uncover its hidden source.

The Creative Inner Child

Children have a wondrous world of creativity. When I ran Inner Child workshops with a colleague many years ago, we held them in a kindergarten. The rooms were always strewn with the creative expression of children's paintings, constructions and other artistry. It always struck me how children have the ability to forego judgement about perspective or appropriate colour; they are more able to engage in the enjoyment of their creative work *for its own sake*. Unfortunately, as we grow into our adult years, we often lose our capacity to be wholly engaged in the enjoyment of the task, without exposure to our own critical filter. We become more attuned to getting it right, and we lose a lot by this focus. It inhibits our enjoyment, and at the end of the day it also restricts our ability to think or develop creatively. We become focussed on the end product rather than wholehearted immersion in the creative experience. How wonderful if we were able to re-claim our Creative Inner Child's perspective.

The Playful Inner Child

This is our sense of fun. It is the part of us that loves a good chuckle, and knows how to extract a feeling of joy from our day-to-day life. It is the part we see in an uninhibited child playing, and we're deprived as adults if we eliminate this aspect from our life. Our Playful Child enhances various aspects of our life, as this facet of our personality can be embedded in many realms, including learning, work, exercise, intimacy, sexuality and friendship. It is important to be able to feel and express our playfulness whether we're three or ninety-three.

When we ran our workshops we included *playtime*, where participants had free reign of the kindergarten. Some people were extremely comfortable, in fact *loved* the opportunity to temporarily relinquish their adult composure and express the playful aspect of their psyche; these people did indeed play. Others were obviously lost and uncomfortable about their ability to do this. Still others played at playing, but were obviously not at home with the experience.

The Spiritual Inner Child

This aspect of our inner world encompasses our sense of awe and wonder, and our sense of *now*. It is about our ability to be in the moment, to feel at one with our world, whether it be through a beautiful sunset, a piece of music that we can feel in our gut, an awareness of the miracle of a young child's emerging development, a connection with another person, or the beauty of a drop of dew on a rose petal. Out Spiritual Inner Child also houses our deep inherent wisdom and the true knowing within each of us and connects us to our own centre and to all around us.

~~

Our Inner Child has our true feelings at its core, and to the degree that we're out of touch with it we're disconnected from our heart's desire and from our own depths. Often when we've been wounded in our early years, we lose touch with these valuable parts of our inner being.

For as long as these aspects of our Inner Child, associated with our *real self*, remains neglected and outside our consciousness, or disowned, we're disadvantaged in our dynamic life journey. To the degree that we can recognise and integrate these vital parts of ourselves, we can live a more full and fruitful life, and we're also freer to enjoy healthy intimacy. I shall say more about this later.

~~

In addition to these aspects of our Inner Child, we've also aspects of our Inner Parent that make up our internal (metaphorical) family. The Inner Parent parts actually are a way of describing our attitude towards our Inner Child. We have come to develop adult mechanisms, both positive and negative. These Inner Parent parts are:

- The Critical Parent
- The Nurturing Parent
- The Protective Parent

The Critical Parent

The Critical Parent is our harsh, judgemental, internal critic, the part that condemns, attacks, and tells us the ways that we don't measure up. It's a voice that most of us recognise, to whatever degree. It's the internal voice that tells us, 'You're too…' or 'You're not…enough', or 'If only you were more…' (fill in the dots!) '…then you'd be okay.'

Initially these judgements came from external sources, most often – but not exclusively – parents. They might have been blatant criticisms; or sometimes they were more subtle. For instance, we may have experienced approval that served as a "reward" for behaving in a particular way. Or sometimes we just picked up on parental expectations. These might have been verbal or non-verbal, explicit or implicit.

Unfortunately, however, external judgements and expectations, regardless of what form they took, are internalised. We can become our own harshest critic, and this is played out in negative self-talk, often outside our conscious awareness. The unrelenting, self-condemning inner judge continually re-plays critical "tapes" of messages. This internal process of self-criticism is the basis of low self-esteem.

We can sometimes recognise the presence of the Critical Parent by starting to pick up on how often our inner voice dictates what we *should* or *shouldn't* be wanting/doing/thinking. What we actually *want* gets lost when we become swamped by the commands of our internal judge. Our real choices are therefore compromised, and we're disempowered at the hand of our own internal attacks.

The Nurturing Parent

Our Nurturing Parent part helps us to be more gentle and compassionate with ourselves, and also more forgiving of our limitations. It is the component of our inner self that is accepting, tolerant, compassionate, and unconditionally loving. We're often able to direct this aspect of ourselves towards others, whether that be towards children, partners or friends. But we might have a lot of difficulty turning these more loving feelings inwards towards ourselves.

The Protective Parent

This is the limit-setting part of our personality. It can work in either direction: *inwardly*, it is the important voice within us that limits and pushes back against the dictates of the Critical Parent. So for instance, if our Critical Parent voice is accusingly telling us, 'You're so lazy!' the Protective push-back voice might be retorting with, 'Hang on, that's not really right. If you're doing something you love doing, you can be up all night working on it. Something else must be going on!' This internal voice gives the Critical Parent voice a run for its money.

The Protective Parent part of our psyche is also very relevant in our *external* world. It is that limit-setting part of us that says 'no' to others when we need to. It helps us to guard ourselves, in a healthy and facilitative way, from those who attempt to violate our boundaries, and from those who try to diminish or undermine us in some way. It is the basis of healthy assertiveness. Hence, it is our Protective Parent that safeguards our Inner Child from the onslaught of destructive authority, both internal and external. It is also the part of us that helps us to extricate ourselves from destructive relationships.

~~

When we look at these three aspects of our Inner Parent, it is important to note that the Nurturing and Protective Parent parts, which are resources within us, work hand in hand, and together form the antidote to the Critical Parent. There is always a direct ratio between the strength of the Critical Parent (our negative self-talk) on the one hand and the strength of the Nurturing and Protective Parents (our self-acceptance and limit-setting internal capabilities) on the other. If the latter two are under-developed or have "gone to sleep", the Critical Parent becomes the boss. In other words, our negative messages to ourselves dominate, and we're left feeling bad about ourselves.

Within the context of our metaphor, the result of the dominance of the Critical Parent is that our Vulnerable Inner Child is overwhelmed with bad feelings. If we've been dominated by the influence of our inner critical voice, and therefor have a low self-esteem, we live with a very fragile Inner Child. The onslaught of internal judgements and attacks leave a heavy imprint. Our self-hate is heightened. If, however, we build on our nurturing and protective resources, the critical voice within us becomes less powerful and influential. It is in this way that we can learn to gradually quieten the harsh dictates of our inner critic, the source of our negative self-talk and the machine that drives our low self-esteem.

It is also extremely important to be able to take ownership of the power of the critical voice within us. It is the fundamental basis of our lack of self-esteem. When we truly recognise that our negative feelings about ourselves stem from our own depths, (rather than being imposed on us from somewhere "out there") we can be empowered in our own healing and in the development of a stronger self-concept. Gradually we can learn to give ourselves a more gentle and loving internal dialogue, rather than the harsh verbal whipping that has often taken place for most of our years.

EXERCISES: (It might be helpful to use a journal to do the exercises that follow through this book, and to keep in touch with how the various concepts in these chapters relate to your life.)

- *How comfortable do you feel with your vulnerable feelings? Do you tend to deny or banish your Vulnerable Inner Child?*
- *How do you feel about your Angry Inner Child?*
    Do you have difficulty owning your angry feelings?
    Do you have difficulty knowing how to constructively express your angry feelings?
- *Are you able to enjoy being playful? When was the last time you enjoyed a good belly laugh? What are some of the ways that you have fun? Could you give yourself permission to do two or three "silly" things in the next week as an expression of your Playful Inner Child?*
- *Are you able to let yourself be fully immersed in the experience of creative activity? Or are you more focussed on being able to produce something "good"?*
- *Do you recognise the feeling of being able to be truly "in the moment"? To fully enjoy that sense of awe and*

wonder? The next time you are walking can you experiment with focusing fully on the things around you, using all your senses: e.g. How many shades of green do you see in the trees and shrubs? What sounds do you hear? Can you hear the birds? What do you smell as you walk? Let your senses be completely alert to the things around you.

- *What are some of the most potent accusations against yourself that stem from your Critical Parent? How do you feel when you experience your attacks against yourself? Can you get a sense of the impact on your Vulnerable Inner Child?*
- *What are some of the ways you nurture yourself? Are you able to be accepting of your limitations?*
- *Are you able to say "no" when you need to? Or to set limits with others about what is acceptable to you?*

Chapter Three
HOW DO WE GO ABOUT CHANGING?

Just as we build relationships in our external world, so we can also build the relationships between aspects of our inner family.

This might feel a little odd to start with. Although we're familiar with the idea of establishing meaningful connections with people we encounter in our day-to-day life, the idea of developing links between aspects of ourselves in our internal world feels less natural. But if we can take this leap of faith and embrace the metaphor, it can be extremely beneficial.

The first thing we need to do is to begin to get a sense of our Inner Child. Sometimes it is helpful initially to think of a child in the external world and how we feel about them. But we need to be able to turn this process inward, and to begin the process of developing a relationship with our own Inner Child.

Following John Bradshaw's example, I often begin this process through a written exercise, which goes as follows:

Think about the child part of you, the part of you that sometimes feels small, hurt, confused, insecure, frightened, or angry. Take a few minutes to think about what you'd like to say to this aspect of you, your Inner Child. But before you do, it's important to be aware how important it is that you never say/write anything to your Inner Child part that's not genuine. Only say things that truly come from your heart; an important part of this process is to start to build an (inner) relationship of trust. It's important in these internal dialogues, just as it is in the relationships you form in your day-to-day life, to do this through always being real with your Inner Child.

When you're ready, write a short letter of just a paragraph or two, telling your inner child whatever you'd like to tell her/him.

Here is an example of what I wrote to my Inner Child. This is just to give you an idea, but be guided by what your heart tells you <u>you</u> want to say to your Inner Child.

> Dear Glennie,
> I know sometimes you feel fragile. I'd like to be able to help you at those times, and to be there for you to develop your strengths. I want you to feel you have my support when you feel sad, insecure, afraid or lonely
> All my love
> Big Glenys.

When you've finished, read your letter slowly, out loud. As you read it, be aware of what you're feeling on the inside.

Now, in a moment I'm going to ask you to write a response from your Inner Child. And this is going to feel really strange, because I'm going to ask you to write it with your non-dominant hand. So if you're right-handed, write your Inner Child's response with your left hand (or vice versa if you're left-handed). The reason for this is that when we write with our dominant hand it calls on the opposite side of the brain, which is the thinking, rational, analytical part. When we switch to the non-dominant hand, it bypasses the thinking, rational part, and goes to the other brain hemisphere, which is the feeling, intuitive part. And our Inner Child speaks the language of feelings.

Be careful of your Critical Parent when you do this exercise. Sometimes when I do these dialogues my letters are back to front. It doesn't matter what your writing is like, and it is important to try not to judge what you are writing. Beware of your critical filter.

Here is an example of my Inner Child's response:

> Dear big Glenys,
> It is so good to hear that and to know I am not alone. I want you to love me just how I am
> Love
> Glennie. ✗✗

When you write your response from your Inner Child to your parent part, don't try to think about what you want to say, just let your pen start rolling across the page. Sometimes you will not expect what your Inner Child writes. Let yourself be surprised!

It's also helpful to just check in with your Inner Child from time to time. Using the same technique, i.e. the dominant/non-dominant hand dialogue, you can write the question:

How are you feeling now?

And then let your Inner Child respond. Remember, the parent part always writes with the dominant hand, the Inner Child with the non-dominant hand.

You might like to continue the dialogue then by responding with something like:

What are you needing from me at the moment?

Again, let your Inner Child respond, using your non-dominant hand.

In this way you are establishing a connection between these inner aspects of yourself and building a basis for the important process of re-parenting.

~~

Apart from the dominant/non-dominant dialogues, another technique I use with clients to help develop the ability to fight back against the Critical Parent is the use of the *empty chair*. This is a method that is often used in Gestalt therapy.

When we use the empty chair technique, we're making more visual and palpable the process that takes place within us. When working with the Critical Parent, I usually do so in the following way:

(1) *Set up three chairs. One of these represents the Critical Parent. One is the Protective Parent. And the third is the Vulnerable Child. The Vulnerable Child is the "victim" of the attacks of the Critical Parent, and can be the default position much of the time.*

(2) *First, sit in the Critical Parent chair. This is one time where I invite people to really go to town with their attacks. Speak out loud all the vitriolic attacks and accusations that usually go on in your head, e.g. 'You're so ugly'. 'Everyone else can find a boyfriend/girlfriend, what's wrong with you?' 'You're so dumb…', etc. For now, do not hold back! Let it flow as viciously as you can.*

(3) *Sit briefly in the Vulnerable Child chair, and check in with how you feel as a consequence of the attack. You may speak if you wish, or you can sit silently and just be aware of how you are feeling.*

(4) *Move to the Protective Parent chair. Feel yourself into the role of the Protective Parent. You may not feel very powerful at this stage, or you may not be sure what to say initially, but start to "push back" and answer the Critical Parent's accusations. Remember, your job is to protect the Inner Child from the onslaught. Be aware how it feels to be in this chair. Defend the Vulnerable Child against the attacks. Feel free to argue with the words of the Critical Parent. For instance, 'He/she is not ugly! Who are you comparing them to? Brad Pitt/Angelina Jolie?' or 'What do you mean he/she's dumb? Look at his/her beautiful art work. 80% is not dumb. And he/she works really hard...' etc.*

(5) *Move back into the Critical Parent chair. Feel yourself into this role now, and respond to the Protective Parent's words.*

(6) *Move back into the Protective Parent chair, and again push back against the words spoken against*

the Inner Child. Don't be afraid to say things like 'I'm not going to let you bully him/her like that', or 'Leave him/her alone! I'm here now to look after him/her, and I won't let you get away with that any longer.'

(7) *Move back and forth between the Critical and Protective Parent chairs, always checking how you are feeling inhabiting that space. Generally, the Critical Parent feels far more powerful in the beginning. But what I almost always find is that people start to feel increasingly stronger in the Protective Parent chair. And once having experienced this in the chair, it becomes somewhat easier to do so within your own head, at least some of the time.*

(8) *When it feels right to leave the exercise for now, move back into the Vulnerable Child chair, and check in with how you are feeling now. Generally, the child part feels increasingly less vulnerable once the experience of the protective resources are utilised in his/her defence.*

~~

Initially it may be difficult for some people to do this exercise on their own. If you have a therapist who is open to this sort of work (but be aware not all would be comfortable working in this modality), the assistance of the therapist may make the exercise easier. Hopefully, once the unfamiliarity of this sort of work becomes less strange, it will prove easier.

Once we get the experience through the empty chair, it often becomes easier to get a "visual feel" for this in our own heads.

~~

A third way of working with the process of connecting with our Inner Child is through a **guided meditation.** I have included an example of the sort of script I might use for this. You could either record this and play it back, or get someone else to read it to you. Or you might be creative enough to conceive your own meditation. I have also utilised John Bradshaw's use of imagining the Inner Child and the Inner Parent. I like to play some soft music in the background for this sort of meditation. I always include an introduction to help relax before the Inner Child visualisation.

Here is a sample of a script you might like to use in this process.

Start by sitting comfortably and quietly. Take a deep breath all the way in, filling your lungs with air. Hold it...and then, as you breathe out, allow the tension to flow out of your body.

Become aware of your surroundings. Feel your body touching the chair. Feel your feet touching the ground. Become aware of any sounds you can hear around you. And let those sounds just be there in the background...you know they're there, but they don't intrude.

And now, let your mind become calm and tranquil, just like the surface of a beautiful, clear lake. If you have interrupting thoughts, that's okay, just allow the thoughts to drift by, like white clouds drifting across a blue sky in your mind, just notice them and allow them to drift by.

Become aware of your breathing. Feel the air in your nostrils, as you breathe in, and as you breathe out. Feel the cool air as you breathe in, and the warm air as you breathe out. And as you breathe, breathe in relaxation, breathe out tension. So with each breath you become more...and more...relaxed.

And as you count backwards from eight to one, allow yourself to be taken deeper and deeper into feelings of calmness and relaxation:

8…7…6…5…deeper and deeper…4…3…2…1. Enjoy the feelings of calmness and relaxation.

And now, in your mind's eye, allow an image to emerge of a place you might have lived in when you were little. It doesn't matter whether it's really where you lived, just let the image emerge as it wants. And as you look around this place in your mind, you become aware of a child. And now, as you move closer, you gradually notice…this is you, as a child!

Notice the surroundings. Are you in a room? Are you outside? Be aware who else might be there with the your younger self, if anyone.

And as you move closer, your adult self looks some more at the child, the young you. Notice how old you are. Now notice how your younger self looks. Happy? Sad?

What else do you notice as you look at your younger self? Your clothes? Your surroundings? Do you notice anything else around you?

What else do you notice about this younger version of you?

Be aware of how your adult self feels as you look at the yourself as a child. Use all of your senses to get a feel for your Inner Child and how being with your younger self impacts on you. What emotional reactions do you notice in yourself as you look down at your younger self? Notice what sensations you feel in your body as you look at that child.

Now you become aware of something the adult you would like to say to your younger self. Imagine yourself telling the child. How does it feel to say that? What do you notice about the child's reaction as you tell them that?

Perhaps you'd like to hold the child? If so, how does it feel to do that? (If you don't want to, don't force yourself, but be aware of how that feels, too.)

Now…feel yourself move into the mind and body of that little child, until you become your younger self.

Be aware of what sorts of feelings and sensations there are in your body as you become the child.

Imagine yourself as the young child looking up at the adult you. What do you see as you look up? How does it feel to look at the adult you?

And now, imagine there is some message you would like to give to the adult you. It might be a question. Or a request. Or any other kind of message.

Imagine now you give that message – in whatever way you like – to the older you. How do you feel as you do that?

Imagine the adult is holding you. How does that feel?

And now, imagine again that you become your adult self as you move into the mind and body of the older you, and you are looking again at the younger you. Is there anything different that you see now looking at the child again?

And now, as you look down, you realise that, for now, it is time to leave. Is there any other message you would like to give that child before you leave? Anything else you want to do before leaving?

Be aware how it feels as you say goodbye and walk away from your younger self. But also be aware that you will be able to return to the child part of you whenever you want. You might even want to reassure the child of this.

And now, having visited your younger self...it is time to return to the present. As you count from one to eight you will start to feel yourself becoming more and more present in the room. 1...2...3...4...5...6...7...8.

Become aware of your surroundings. Feel your body touching the chair. Feel your feel touching the ground. Be aware of any sounds you hear around you.

Feeling relaxed but refreshed and alert, it is time to gently return to your normal waking consciousness, be fully present in the room, and…when you're ready…slowly…open your eyes.

~~

These three methods are useful in helping us to make the metaphor of the Inner Child more "tangible" in the process of re-parenting ourselves. And it is through the process of re-parenting that we can gradually re-frame the old negative messages that we internalised from our earlier life. By learning to build and rely on the nurturing and protective adult resources within us, we can change the tendency for our critical attacks on ourselves to dominate our psyche. Hence we start to slow the tide of negative self-talk that feeds into our low self-esteem.

Chapter Four
IDEALIZED IMAGES

Our feelings of inadequacy generally begin early in our lives. We may have experienced this as having been a shy child. Or we may remember having been afraid to put our hand up when the teacher asked questions, even if we know the answer. On the other hand, our lack of confidence might have been disguised under a façade of bravado or rebellion, often hidden not only from others but also from ourselves.

We develop an array of beliefs, assumptions and behaviours that aren't helpful. One of the typical tendencies that emerge from feelings of inadequacy is to construct what are sometimes called *idealised images*. Because we don't believe we're *intrinsically* worthwhile, we look for external ways of measuring our value. A substitute for self-esteem, an idealised image is a picture of what we believe we need to be in order to feel that we're okay.

So we develop an internal standard or expectation. For example, we might believe that if only we were smart enough, or attractive enough, or had a boyfriend/girlfriend, *then* we would be okay. It is an inner expectation of what we think we *should* be in order to be worthwhile. But if we believe we have to be something other than what we are, we fail to accept and validate what we *actually* are.

Sometimes we may compare ourselves with an actual person. If, for example, we compare our body shape to an actor or model, or to a slim friend, we may tell ourselves that we're too fat, even if that is not objectively real. So we believe that we don't measure up. At its worst our relationship to our body can culminate in distortions of body image, where a slim person sees themselves as much larger than they really are. I have sometimes asked a client to draw a picture of how they see themselves, and in some instances their perception bears no relationship to reality.

Sometimes we grow up in the shadow of a parent or a sibling, and this might form the basis of an idealised image. If that parent or sibling is extremely clever or good looking, or has achieved notoriety or success in some field, we may compare ourselves negatively, and believe that we are therefore not as worthwhile. Parents sometimes feed into this by referring to a sibling as *the pretty/good looking one* or *the smart one*. We might therefore find ourselves wanting.

Parents can be unaware of the lasting psychological impact these descriptors have on their offspring. I often see people in my practice who are well advanced in years, but who still carry the traces of these comments in their psyche. The old parental messages might now be internalised, and the Critical Parent voice within now tells us that we're not clever enough, or not pretty/good looking enough; therefore we hold an assumption we don't measure up. So, many years after the idealised images were originally created, the effects of the old messages are still potent, and our Vulnerable Inner Child is still battered by these harsh messages.

Often we expend a lot of energy trying to live up to our idealised images. So, for instance, if we don't believe in our inner worth, we may have an idealised image about wealth. We might tell ourselves, 'If I had one million dollars I will have proven myself, and I will therefore feel okay.' So we might work hard to achieve this goal. And if we don't live up to this, we sink into more self-condemnation, and feel even worse.

But if we do achieve our idealised image, we might get what I call "the ten second buzz". For a brief period of time we might feel okay about ourselves. However if we don't have a real belief that we're inherently worthwhile, this "buzz" cannot last. And so we will just lift the bar. Since one million didn't do it, we may strive for two million, or five…and so it continues. The bar keeps getting lifted, without the desired result. Unless we feel good enough about ourselves *intrinsically* we will continue to search for *external* proof of our worth. It doesn't work in the long term, since our Critical

Parent voice will continue to give us the message, 'You're just not good enough'. And our Vulnerable Inner Child will continue to feel bad or inadequate. The message we're giving ourselves is that we need to be different. And if we believe we have to be something other than what we are, we fail to accept and validate what we in fact are.

Fortunately this situation does not have to be sustained. When we were young all we had was our "vulnerable child" part. But as adults when we feel vulnerable, although we might *feel* as if all we have is our Vulnerable Inner Child, in fact we can also draw on our adult resources: we now have our Nurturing Parent and our Protective Parent parts. Through re-parenting ourselves, i.e. utilising these adult strengths, we can begin the process of developing a healthier self-esteem. We can push back against the power of the old messages that have been held for so long, and start to develop different assumptions about ourselves.

Although it may feel daunting initially, it can be very liberating to let go of our idealised images, the expectations we've previously held and identified with.

This doesn't mean we don't have goals. It's important for us to be able to strive for things that are important to us. But if we check in with ourselves and recognise that our worth is on the line, that is, that we'll feel worthwhile if we succeed and deride ourselves and feel bad if we don't, we can assume that what we're striving for is an idealised image. Our idealised images constitute part of our persona, in the masks we've adopted. They're not part of our real self, the part of us that will ultimately feel like we've come home, attached to our own centre.

~~

EXERCISES:

- ***Write a list of any idealised images you have adopted for yourself through your life. Can you recognise the Critical Parent messages/attacks on yourself relating to these idealised images? e.g. 'You're so dumb!' or 'You're too fat!' etc.***
- ***How do these idealised images and associated Critical Parent accusations impact on your life? And on the pressure you put on yourself to be your idealised self?***

Chapter Five
GETTING IN OUR OWN WAY

I have found that it's not unusual for people who engage in therapy to become impatient. This is understandable; after all, they have come along to feel better, and sometimes it can be frustrating to find that after hearing and learning what can happen things don't immediately change. It takes time. We usually know at a *thinking* level a considerable time before we acquire that knowing at a *feeling* level. We need to wait for our heart to catch up with our head, in its own time; and it is a very different experience when we *feel* the change. But we can't push the fast-forward button. It takes as long as it takes. Or as I once heard it said, 'We do what we do till we don't'.

So how come our psyche is so resistant to change? One way we can understand this is to look at a quote by American psychologist Virginia Satir, who said, "Most people prefer the certainty of misery to the misery of uncertainty". My understanding of this is that we tend to cling to patterns or beliefs that have become automatic and habitual, no matter how destructive or painful they may be.

Why do we do this? Because these patterns are familiar, and we're more comfortable with what is familiar, even when our patterns are painful or destructive. Change is initially uncomfortable, so we don't relish the *misery of uncertainty*. We tend to automatically slide into the deeply etched groove, the familiar *certainty of misery*. It's like a magnet that draws us back. Over time it has become our default position. But the work of therapy, or indeed any change, is to gradually move into unfamiliar and more fruitful territory that ultimately will become more familiar over time, in spite of the early discomfort.

A small example of this is if we have low self-esteem and are entrenched in a high level of negative self-talk, in alliance with the messages from our inner Critical Parent. It might seem natural that we would then love to hear more positive things about ourselves from others. But, interestingly, if someone gives us a compliment we might feel uneasy, and will often try to bat the positive words away with a 'yes but…', or dismiss them altogether, because the words we're hearing are not congruent with what we've always believed about ourselves.

In fact, if we have a negative view of ourselves our antennae will be up and out, looking for confirmation of what we've always believed. We *prefer the certainty of misery to the misery of uncertainty*. Over time we need to develop a more positive assumption about ourselves, gradually allowing it to become more familiar and accepted by us.

~~

Any shift needs to be a process over time, in small increments. In any change, if we step just slightly outside our comfort zone, into the unfamiliar, we'll feel a little anxiety; but if we can let ourselves just sit with this (low) level of anxiety for a while, we accommodate it, and it becomes more tolerable. So in the example above, instead of brushing away a compliment because if feels uncomfortable, it is helpful to just say 'thank you' and sit with any slight discomfort we might feel, even if we don't initially believe what we're being told. We need to be able to let the positive message in, just a little.

By sitting with this low level of anxiety, we will have expanded our band of comfort. And so we step just outside our comfort zone, again, and again. We're thus enabling ourselves to tolerate more of what initially felt uncomfortable, our *misery of uncertainty*.

However, when we're engaging in the process of changing our old, ingrained patterns it's important not to step too far from the familiar *too* quickly, or we'll scare ourselves silly. Remembering that many of the patterns that are associated with our *certainty of misery* were those that were put in place as children in order to help us to survive emotionally, letting go of those old habits can't be undertaken all at once, as it would expose us too suddenly to the full thrust of our internal basic anxiety, and we would feel at some deep unconscious level as if our very survival was under threat.

If we've lived with low self-esteem, the underpinnings – our Critical Parent accusations – have become part of our *certainty of misery*. It is bound to take time for us to turn this around. We sometimes feel disheartened about this. Because it doesn't happen quickly, we believe that it cannot happen at all. We assume that because "so it has been, so it is…then so it must always be". We can't change the first two aspects of this triad; but we can change how it can be in the future; however, we need to be patient with ourselves.

It is interesting to reflect, too, in line with the increased understanding of brain plasticity, how in time the neural pathways can change. Physiologically, we can also move from what has been habitual to a new way of being.

EXERCISES:

- *Can you think which assumptions/attitudes/habits have become part of your "certainty of misery", i.e.*

patterns that have become familiar, but which may be painful or destructive?

- *Can you think of any ways you experience the "misery of uncertainty" when you've felt deviations from these old patterns?*
- *What ways might you try stepping outside your comfort zone? Trying something different? Taking a few new risks? How does it feel when you try these steps?*

Chapter Six
PROJECTIONS

One of the important aspects of healing our low self-esteem is to recognise and take ownership of our projections. When we talk about projections in this context we're looking at an unconscious psychological mechanism.

A way of understanding this is to think of a film projector, and a screen. The film is fed through a projector, and is reflected onto the screen. A similar mechanism happens with our own projections. We have our inner thoughts and assumptions. If we think about the powerful effects of our Critical Parent, and take into account how we're affected by our internal accusations and judgements, we know we can often feel really bad, even self-hating. And sometimes, at a deep level, our psyche knows that it is too painful for us to hold these feelings. So we unconsciously project our negative judgements onto others.

We can do this in one of two ways: either

(1) we transfer our judgements of ourselves onto others, and so become critical of them, or

(2) we think other people are judging us.

Of course, sometimes others *may* be critical of us. But whether they are or not, unless that is spelled out to us we don't really know what they are thinking. We assume, because we've projected our own self-criticism, that the criticism comes from someone else. But the judgements that we assume are being directed towards us by others are usually grounded within ourselves.

It can be quite empowering to be able to relocate the source of our negative judgements. We feel more at the mercy of others if we believe *they* are critical of us, and that the measure of our worth is dependent on how they see us. But when we're able to own our projections, and know these arrows are fired by *our own* internal Critical Parent rather than by someone else, we can ultimately find ways to stop injuring ourselves, through the process of re-parenting, by giving "muscle" to our Nurturing Parent and our Protective Parent, and by utilising these strengths within us to fight back against the might of our own harsh inner critical voice.

So recognising and owning our critical projections is a powerful aid in the path to better self-esteem. For as long as we believe our bad feelings "invade" us from outside, we feel in the hands of something we can't do anything about. Once we identify that *we ourselves* are the source of those bad feelings, that it is our own negative self-talk that has, through projection, unconsciously been falsely re-directed and attributed to others, we've enabled ourselves on the path to feeling more comfortable in our own skin. True, it's only the beginning, but that's the only place we can start. It is possible then to start the process of fighting back with the assistance of the nurturing and protective resources that also lie within us. The more we develop these resources, the less the Critical Parent voice can dominate.

Sometimes we build elaborate stories about what we imagine other people are thinking about us. It can feel very real. As we've seen, projections can be very powerful. However, it can be helpful to recognise that not everyone is always thinking about us in the way we imagine. Whilst we might have fantasies, through our projections, that they are thinking all sorts of negative things, in reality they might be wondering what's for dinner, or wondering what they are going to wear to the party on Saturday night. Or – and here's a radical thought – they might even be thinking something positive about us… *if* they have us in their mind at all!

Moreover, if it were not for our own critical voice, we would not react in the same way, even if someone were judging us. We'd be more able to simply question whether the comment or thought fitted for us, or not. If we decided it didn't fit, we'd be able to just let it go. If it did, we might be able to take it on board, without judging ourselves harshly.

I remember a woman in one of my groups many years ago encapsulating this well, when she said, 'You know, if someone calls me a pink-spotted butterfly, it's not going to bother me, because I know I'm not a pink-spotted butterfly.' If someone is critical of us, or we perceive them to be, it will not wound us so deeply, unless it is congruent with a critical part of ourselves.

EXERCISES:

- *Can you think of times you've projected your Critical Parent onto others?*
- *Do you tend more to become critical of others? Or see them as critical of you?*
- *When you next believe someone is thinking something negative of you, check in with yourself if there is actual evidence of this. Might it actually be your own negative beliefs? How does it feel to re-frame this?*

Chapter Seven
CORE ISSUES

We've seen how the wounds of childhood will play themselves out in various ways as we move beyond our early developmental years. The "shape" in which these wounds are experienced subsequently, often continuing well into our adult years, will depend on the particular nature of our environmental influences. In many instances the after-effects will impact on our level of self-esteem, as the scales are tipped more in the direction of internal, deeply-etched anxiety rather than in a trust in ourselves and our world.

It's helpful to be able to identify the core issue(s) we experienced during these formative developmental stages of life, as well as the ways we adapt to them. These core issues have been called "life themes" by Daphne Kingma (*Finding True Love*). We may have experienced two or several of these core issues, which are often linked. They include: neglect, separation, loss, poverty, abuse, abandonment, rejection, emotional smothering or overprotection, family patterns of illness, feelings of not belonging, parental criticism or expectations, lack of validation or invalidation, fear of annihilation (fear for our very existence).

Neglect: This can, of course, take many forms. There's the more blatant form of neglect, where our basic physical needs aren't met, for instance our need to be adequately fed, clothed according to temperature, and kept safe.

Or we can be neglected in less obvious ways, where our emotional needs are not attended to appropriately. This is often obscured from our conscious awareness, because we assume, since our basic physical needs have been satisfied, that we were cared for, and that we had "a happy childhood". But some part of our being registers that we've missed out on the important emotional components.

Each of these kinds of neglect can have a long-lasting impact on our well-being and can contribute to our deep basic anxiety which will be at the cost of a real sense of our intrinsic worth. As very young children, even at a pre-verbal stage, we can begin to have the long-lasting sense that there must be something wrong with us if Mum or Dad could not be there for us in the way we needed them to be. As adults, we sometimes live with an abiding sense of guilt: the child that still dwells within us might continue to carry the feeling that things must be our fault. This will inevitably effect our level of self-esteem.

Separation: If circumstances led to a separation from our caregiver(s) during our early years, this can contribute to significant insecurity both as children and later on in our adult years. This can happen when one or both parents were not present when we needed them to be.

> *Claire is a forty-year-old, who came to see me for anxiety and depression. She'd always suffered with a lack of belief in herself.*
>
> *When she was five years old she was involved in an accident where a car hit her, and she was subsequently hospitalised for several weeks. During Claire's very long, traumatic experience away from home, her mother rarely visited her. It was only when she was much older she learned that at that time her mother had been going through a nervous breakdown.*
>
> *Being hospitalised as little children can be very scary. We need our parents there to comfort us. Consequently, although Claire's mother had her own reasons for not being present to support her through this very anxiety-provoking experience, at a deep unconscious level the little girl came to believe that there was something about her that didn't deserve to be loved; she was left with many negative feelings about herself. This early trauma continued to impact her significantly well into her adult years, when she struggled with feelings of not really being lovable enough.*

Another example of separation as a critical core issue is when it's Mum who goes into hospital, perhaps to have another baby, or because she's ill. As children we're so dependant and can feel the absence acutely. This, too, can sometimes have a lasting impact.

Whatever, the reason, if the separation feels traumatic, a secure sense of self can be compromised in ensuing years. The child/adult can be left with a deep-seated sense of "there must be something about me". At an unconscious level there is a fantasy that if we'd been good/worthy enough our parent would have been there for us.

Loss: The death of a significant person, most markedly a parent, or their departure from our life when we were young can, of course, have a profound effect on our sense of security.

Separation and divorce can also lead to a great sense of loss. How that loss was handled is very important. It needs to be done sensitively. But the emotional barbs that often accompany divorce have sometimes impacted on us; as adults we can even be left wary of forming close bonds with others. In some instances we might even have irrationally felt it was our fault the loss occurred.

Poverty: if we've grown up in a family where poverty has prevailed this can influence our attitudes to money, or whatever it symbolises for us, in our adult years.

Cathy is a fifty-five year old woman who works as a manager in a large corporation. She earns a large salary. However, she constantly lives with a fear she will not have enough money. She lives frugally, despite her high income. Her memories associated with childhood where she constantly saw her parents having to scrimp for food, have had a lasting impact. She now has an abiding sense that she will not feel okay until she has reached a certain level of wealth.

We can see in this example how fears associated with fiscal security can come to dominate our thoughts, sometimes manifesting in an idealised image associated with wealth. Our sense of worth might therefore be challenged by threats of not having enough financial value.

Money may also come to be symbolically associated with internal resources: we might develop a fear that we've not got enough within us to manage.

Abuse: This can take many forms. We might have suffered physical or sexual abuse. Or it could have been psychological/emotional abuse, which can be less obvious but not necessarily less potent. For example, if someone taunts, bullies, derides, or deliberately confuses us, these can be forms of emotional abuse. Or there may be manipulation through power, such as withholding money or affection.

Each of these forms of abuse can leave us with a doubt about our worth. In fact, this is something I frequently evidence with clients, who unfortunately are left with a feeling of self-blame or guilt about something they had no control over at a vulnerable stage of life. This feeds into low self-esteem, under the auspices of the Critical Parent.

Abandonment: Again, this can relate to either a physical abandonment, for example if a parent left home and never saw us again, *or* emotional unavailability of one or both parents. In the latter instance our parent(s) may have fulfilled our practical, physical needs but may have been unable to provide us with the important emotional connection and support we needed.

Even if there were reasons for either form of abandonment, as little children we could not have understood this. Abandonment is a form of loss, which can also leave us insecure about our worth.

Rejection: We may have experienced rejection of a blatant kind, e.g. if Dad wanted a son who was sporty and athletic, he may have derided his more artistic and sensitive boy, or scorned his interests. Or the children at school may have rejected us because we wore thick glasses or spoke with an accent. In other instances rejection may have been more subtle. We might have found that we were always among the last to be picked for a sport's team.

Whatever its form, rejection might have left us with a general feeling of unacceptability, or a sense that we're not likable/lovable.

Emotional Smothering or Overprotection: This can sometimes be difficult to recognise, because the behaviour of a parent is so encased in an apparently "loving" form.

We all need to be protected when we're little. But if our parent(s) tended to *over*protect us, we might never have learned that we were capable of looking after ourselves. Sometimes our parents, through their own anxiety, are afraid to allow or encourage us to become independent of them. For instance, they might not allow us to start to venture beyond the family circle. Autonomous activities, or engaging in social events with peers, and learning to make our own way to places rather than always being accompanied by a parent, is a normal part of development once we reach an appropriate age. But a parent's anxiety may impel them to check up on our activities and emotional reactions, in a more extreme way than is helpful, and so keep us enmeshed and less emotionally separate than we need to be. So because of her own anxieties and lack of firm boundaries, mother might have smothered us, or perhaps treated us as if we were an extension of her. We were therefore left with a sense that we are not whole and separate. Our belief in ourselves will have been compromised, and our sense of trust in our own competence undermined, albeit unwittingly.

Family Patterns of Illness: If a parent was depressed, or always confined to bed for some other form of illness, this can impact on our ensuing confidence. A depressed mother/father can't be as fully available to us emotionally as we need. Physical illness, although unavoidable, can have similar ramifications for us as children if our natural needs aren't adequately fulfilled.

Feelings of Not Belonging: We might have grown up feeling we were "different" in some way, either because of cultural differences (e.g. a migrant who did not speak the language), or sometimes physical or other differences. Or there may have been a sense of having been ostracised within the family for some reason.

A sense of belonging is very important. Our feelings of isolation or not belonging can also leave us with a sense that there is something amiss with us.

Parental Criticism or Expectations: We've looked at the impact of these tendencies. They form the basis of our internalised Critical Parent, the basis of our low self-esteem.

Lack of Validation, or Invalidation: It's vital that we have a sense of validation, i.e. "I see you, I hear you, I take you seriously". Validation gives us a sense that it is important what we think, and it is important what we feel. If we don't experience this in our childhood, we can grow up not trusting our thoughts and feelings, an essential ingredient of self-esteem.

> *Susan grew up in a family where she was never encouraged or allowed to value her own thoughts and emotions. Her parents tended to tell her what she should or shouldn't be feeling. 'You shouldn't get angry', or 'You should be grateful for what Hilary does for you;, or 'Don't get upset', etc. If she cried she was told, 'I'll give you something to really cry about'. When situations arose where Susan confided in her parents about events in her life they would emphatically tell her what she should say or what she should do.*
>
> *This intrusion on Susan's natural emotional experience was psychologically destructive, since she ultimately was left not really*

knowing what she felt or thought. Her sense of self was significantly compromised.

Fear for our Existence, Fear of Annihilation: In our earliest years, if our caregiver isn't available when we need them, even if inadvertently – Mum may be busy with five other children – inaccessibility to our needs may feel terrifying: we unconsciously come to fear for our very existence, since we're totally dependent on our caregiver for our survival. Our sense of security is thus threatened.

This can be echoed in our adult life when situations or events in our environment unconsciously trigger the old feelings, and the primitive fear is revived.

Sandy is a thirty-five year old woman. She had been in therapy for six months, dealing with self-esteem issues. We had uncovered details of her childhood; she had discovered that her mother had suicided when she was just three months old. We had looked at how this would have presented a profound loss and early trauma for the young, totally dependent infant at this vulnerable stage of her life. Her father, who busied himself at work and was also emotionally absent, had enlisted the assistance of his mother, who was a distant, cold woman.

Sandy, who had been married for ten years, now felt very dependent on her husband for emotional support. In recent sessions she had been talking about his busy work schedule, and how he was coming home increasingly late. One day in her sessions she was particularly visibly distressed, and started to talk about how she feared he might be having an affair. As she talked about her high level of anxiety she started to report feeing shaky, "as if she was cold", although the temperature was in fact very warm that day. She was experiencing a form of primitive anxiety, or what is also called "catastrophic anxiety" – a fear for her very existence. The childhood fears that she could not exist, which would have accompanied the loss of her mother at such a young stage of her life, had resurfaced with the fear that her husband might not be there for her.

~~

Since each of these core issues can impede caregivers' ability to meet our early dependency needs, they can feed into later self-esteem difficulties. They might also have unconsciously contributed to our belief that these experiences with our caregivers were our fault.

EXERCISES:

- *Can you identify your core issue(s)? How have they influenced your life as an adult?*
- *Can you see how they might have affected your self-esteem?*

Chapter Eight
COMPROMISING AND ADAPTING TO OUR CORE ISSUES

As we've seen, as young children we will have adapted to our environmental difficulties in order to survive emotionally. The particular pattern we choose (unconsciously), or the masks we put in place, will be dependent on the nature of our environment, i.e. the type of core issue(s) we have encountered, primarily in our family-of-origin, as well as in our extended environment, like school and peers.

The impact of these early hurdles can be quite profound. As adults, we'll be emotionally sensitive to anything associated with our core issues. Whilst others might have mild responses to a particular situation, if something taps into our old childhood experiences we'll have a much stronger reaction. This is why we may sometimes seem to "over-react". For example, our buttons might be pushed if our partner wants to know where we're going and what we're doing, because it (unconsciously) reminds us of our experience of being emotionally smothered as a child. Or we may be prone to particularly strong emotional responses if someone is late; our childhood experience of abandonment may trigger a hidden fear we've been abandoned again.

Our old insecurities are stirred up again in our adult years. We can feel very raw around reminders of our core issue(s). We might therefore have found ways to adapt, in order to avoid feeling the old uncomfortable emotions experienced through the early occurrences. Our *adaptations* (which are the ways we cope with our core issues) are the patterns that are put in place to protect us in those early years. These adaptations, outlined by Daphne Kingma in her book, might include: compliance, defiance, becoming an over-achiever, or an under-achiever, perfectionism, emotional dependence, withdrawal, commitment phobia, passive-aggression, depression, addiction, co-dependency, over-intellectualisation, or manipulativeness.

Compliance: Compliant tendencies are usually the hallmark of the "good girl/boy". We learned to become people-pleasers, a bit like chameleons, changing our ways according to what we felt might bring us approval. Sadly, as little children we may have come to believe we could only get the acceptance or love we longed for by adapting to what we thought others wanted us to do/think/feel. This adaptation will often follow themes like loss, abandonment, lack of validation, or early rejection.

Defiance (Rebelliousness): Adapting to an environment where we felt the expectations of our parents and others, we learned to dig our heels in and react in opposition to what was demanded of us.

Unfortunately, whether we're compliant or defiant, this is at a cost of real autonomy: we're acting in response to the other person, either by adapting to what we know/believe they want, or in opposition to them. We do this at the cost of coming from our own centre, where we act according to our own truth. If we're most often *reacting* in response to others rather than *acting* from our real self, it will erode our sense of self and our ability to assert ourselves effectively.

Becoming an Over-achiever: Following on from what we felt to be expectations from parents or others, we may have habitually come to believe that in order to be okay we had to constantly prove ourselves through achieving. Achievement became our idealised image.

Perfectionism: This adaptation can be linked with over-achievement. Since we can only feel a sense of worth through doing well, we keep trying to prove ourselves by continually raising the bar.

Becoming an Under-achiever: this can stem from a belief that achievement is out of our reach, and it's deemed better not to try something for fear of not being able to succeed. This adaptation can also come out of criticism or expectations - implicit or explicit - during our early years.

Emotional Dependence: Many core issues can result in this way of dealing with our insecurities. With our childhood dependency needs not being adequately met because of abandonment, neglect, separation, rejection, lack of validation, etc., our self-confidence and our ability to emotionally care for ourselves have been diminished, and we believe it is only through someone else we can manage. We might think that others can fill the internal gaping hole of insecurity. Of course this leaves us very vulnerable to the attitudes of others towards us. The measure of our worth has been externalised.

Withdrawal: This adaptation to our pain suggests a sense of hopelessness. In our early years the world seemed like an unfriendly or scary place, and so we learned to isolate ourselves as a way of distancing from an environment that felt unsafe. It's as if we wear a suit of armour to protect us. We've come to believe if we detach then we cannot be hurt. The detachment can be from other people, or from our own feelings.

Abuse or abandonment are examples of core issues that can cause us to withdraw emotionally.

Commitment Phobia: To commit in a relationship requires an open heart. But when we open our heart we can never have absolute guarantees, and we are therefore exposed to our vulnerability. As soon as we start to feel any "threat" of attachment, we might therefore want to pull back. We don't trust that we have the strength to survive the necessary vulnerability associated with attachment to someone.

This adaptation can also stem from an early over-protectiveness, and a fear of being smothered again in our adult relationships. Or it may derive from an environment where our emotional needs were neglected, and so we fear exposure to such vulnerability again.

Passive-aggression: if we're not comfortable with expressing our angry feelings overtly, we might instead express them in more covert ways. The tendency to submerge angry emotions means they sometimes sneak out unconsciously in other forms. For instance, we might always be late, or we might refuse to engage in emotional discussion, and instead hide behind a newspaper or TV, or walk out of the room.

Perhaps this comes out of a *fear* of our angry feelings because we experienced abuse as children; hence we've come to be afraid that our own anger might explode in the same manner. Or perhaps our angry feelings were not permitted or validated in our younger years, so we learned to disguise them.

Depression: This can be as a result of most of the early core issues not being resolved. The unfinished business of the past keeps simmering under the surface, and we can't feel fulfilled or at peace with ourselves under these circumstances.

Or sometimes the failure to be able to express anger outwardly leads to the emotion being aimed inward: our aggression is directed against ourselves, and converts to depression.

Addiction: This adaptation can take many forms, like alcohol, drugs, gambling, shopping, sex, compulsive eating, smoking, and other forms of behaviour. It can come out of our woundedness, as experienced via our core issues, stemming from a dysfunctional family history. Addictions can also be a way of trying to suppress the intensity of our deep anxiety deriving from our early negative environmental influences.

Co-dependency: This adaptation is associated with a dysfunctional dependence within an intimate relationship in which we prioritise the other's needs at the cost of our own. If we're co-dependent we'll often choose a relationship in which we support or enable either addiction or mental health problems, often acting as the "rescuer". Because this may help us feel needed, we're dependent on something or someone outside ourselves for our sense of purpose or worth. Other typical hallmarks of co-dependency include low self-esteem and a inclination to people-pleasing, as well as poor boundaries (i.e. we have difficulty differentiating what thoughts/feelings belong with us and what belongs with the other person, and thus where responsibility for a problem/situation lies).

Over-intellectualisation: This is a defence mechanism developed to distance ourselves from emotions. Sometimes it might feel safer to reside in our thoughts and minds than to expose ourselves to the seemingly vulnerable world of feelings. If we were not emotionally "held" enough in our formative years when we were vulnerable, we might have adapted in this way, choosing a pseudo-objective approach rather than risking exposure to pain. Our earlier fear of not being able to manage those feelings has been carried through to our adult years.

Manipulativeness: This is a covert means of trying to change another person's beliefs, emotions or behaviour to advance our own interests. It's often linked with a need to feel in control in order to promote our self-esteem.

~~

As we saw earlier, these adaptations are some of the patterns or masks that we developed in order to survive in our immature years. They are closely linked to our self-esteem. Through these adaptations our Inner Child has learned to become *who we think we need to be* in order to survive. But these adaptations incur a high cost: our sense of *who we really are*. We abandon aspects of our real self in favour of a false self or persona. This process is not usually in our conscious awareness.

Our challenge and our growing edge is, of course, to gradually learn to accept who we really are, with our complete package of strengths and limitations. As we've seen, the process of re-parenting is a conduit to achieving this goal. Through this method we learn to push back against our internal dictates to be other than our real self.

EXERCISES:

- *Which adaptations have you utilised in order to try to overcome the influence of your core issues?*
- *How have these adaptations affected your wellbeing in life? Can you see ways they might have inhibited authentic self-esteem?*

Chapter Nine
RELATIONSHIPS AND SELF-ESTEEM

We often hear it said that we need to love ourselves in order to be loved. What does this really mean?

How we feel about ourselves, as a consequence of our past, is an important facet of adult relating. Unless we have a reasonable level of self-regard, we can't be open to the whole spectrum of possibilities of a loving relationship with a partner. Rather, the relationship will be coloured by expectations, albeit unconscious, that the other person provides us with *what we can't provide for ourselves:* a deep-seated conviction that we're lovable. If we don't love ourselves, we are at risk of expecting our partner to provide us with a belief in ourselves.

Although we all like to feel safe and loved, and to have affirmation of our worth, this needs to be the icing on the cake rather than the cake itself. Otherwise expectations are likely to put pressure on the quality of the relationship. And, in fact, we render ourselves at risk if we're dependent on someone else for a belief in our value, for we're then slaves to their perceptions of us: we're tossed from the heights of their belief we're worthwhile to the depths of despair when we're criticised or held in low esteem. A stable sense of our worth can only be held when our relationship with ourselves is fundamentally positive and we have a belief that our real self is lovable.

If a relationship is to be fulfilling, it's important that we're able to *be* our real selves (after all, we want to be loved for who we really are). Remembering that our adaptations compromise our real self, our ability to relate authentically and autonomously will have been impaired. If we're relating to another person through the medium of adaptations and masks, our sense of self and our boundaries are weakened. Our compliance defiance, perfectionism, commitment phobia, withdrawal, passive-aggression, emotional dependency, addictions, etc., are likely to impact on our relationship with our partner, because they impact on our relationship with ourselves. We can't be authentic and whole if we're struggling with trying to be someone else, or we're struggling to prove ourselves. We are operating from our persona/false self.

In addition, the less we're our real selves in relationship, the more likely that connection is contaminated by projections and idealised images. We're likely to idealise partners, often unconsciously projecting onto them the positive attributes we would like to find; or we may project negative aspects onto them and so perceive them, for example, as if *they* were a critical parent.

However, to the extent we do this, we unconsciously relate to our projections and idealisations of the other person, rather than to the real person. The same can be happening towards us too, of course.

The experience of intimacy is the place within which we want and need to feel most safe, yet, by its very nature, it's often where we feel most vulnerable. And, of course, it's inevitable that there will be some degree of vulnerability when we open ourselves to loving and caring for another human being. Intimacy and closeness means opening our hearts to love in a context that can have no absolute certainty. We're consequently bound to have a level of vulnerability, even in the most healthy, secure relationship. And we'll be most emotionally exposed and reactive to the events and situations that are associated with our core issues and adaptations.

Deep in our unconscious, our present day relationships are coloured by the experiences of old relationships, in particular our earliest, consciously forgotten experience of intimacy as a *totally dependent chid*. Our parents generally constitute our earliest experience of intimacy. Even where there has been "good enough" parenting during childhood, we can't escape the vulnerable feelings, which will emerge again in our adult relationships. So our core childhood issues are likely to re-surface: our buttons will be pushed more in the context of adult intimacy than in any other, because it's the place where we're the most emotionally naked. It's therefore important that we become aware of the unresolved aspects of our past experience that might be influencing our here-and-now relationships.

For a relationship to be maximally healthy and fulfilling, we need to have two whole, autonomous people relating authentically to each other, real self to real self. I remember once being told of a wonderful metaphor for such a relationship: it's like two fried eggs, where the eggs are joined, but the yolks are separate. In a healthy relationship there is closeness and joining on the one hand (the fried eggs), but with the simultaneous maintenance of two whole, autonomous individuals with clear boundaries who relate at an intimate level (the yolks).

By boundaries, I'm referring to a clear awareness of what belongs where: being able to separate responsibility for our own thoughts, feelings or needs from another person's. It also means we're not responsible for fixing the other person's difficulties, nor are they for ours. This doesn't mean a lack of care of compassion, but the ultimate responsibility for each individual lies within their own self-boundaries.

We're responsible for our belief in our worth. This essentially needs to be an internal process, and it is possible through what we've described earlier as re-parenting.

Unfortunately, in many relationships boundaries are not so clear. Too often, closeness is confused with a boundary-less merging, in which each person blends imperceptibly with the other; each partner may feel responsible for the other's problems and wellbeing – the "egg yolks" are runny, without a real defining psychological distinction between one and the other.

Whilst at a surface level this type of "closeness" may feel good, and allay the anxiety we may have of isolation, or of our existential aloneness, it's ultimately not satisfying at a deeper level. At this depth, the price to be paid is a compromise of self. One or both may eventually experience a feeling of being taken over by the other, or a feeling of having lost a sense of "selfhood". And indeed, this sadly does often occur; there's often an absence of a real *knowing* of our *self* in such a situation, because our self has been rendered subservient, or negated, in the context of an enmeshed relationship. This is usually associated with the remnants of unfinished business deriving from the core issues of our childhood.

Tracey was an insecure woman of fifty when she met Bruce. She was a couple of years out of a long marriage, and just starting to venture into the singles scene. He was an interestingly eccentric and charming man, whom she was immediately drawn to. He introduced her to many new life experiences, and many interesting people. These were awakenings to the rather timid woman.

Bruce was inclined to control her in his own charming way. This dovetailed with Tracey's compliant and accommodating personality, a pattern stemming from early childhood, when she lived in the shadow of her loving but dominant parents. At that young age she'd learned to win approval from her parents through her submission to their wishes and beliefs. Subsequently in her relationships Tracey had then tended to compromise herself and merge with powerful personalities like Bruce.

She'd not really developed a secure sense of herself in her family-of-origin environment, so it was easy for her to slip into this old pattern with him. She soon lost her self in the relationship, and didn't really take into account what she wanted or needed.

Sometimes she would leave him when her was in a good mood, and come back some time later to find that he'd shifted into a black mood. Since Tracey didn't have the confidence to hold onto her sense of her own separateness and autonomy in the context of the relationship, she blamed herself and automatically assumed she must be responsible for Bruce's bad mood, and in order to try to "fix" things up (which of course she could never have done anyway!) she'd attempt to console, placate, or just get out of the way, whilst inside she felt confused, insecure, rejected, guilty, unloved and unlovable.

Her subsequent therapy helped her to understand that Bruce's emotions were not her responsibility, and in fact had little to do with her. In the course of time she learned to connect with her own centre rather than take her bearings from outside herself. She also worked to build her self-esteem (through developing more muscle to her Nurturing Parent and Protective Parent), which also helped her to set limits with Bruce! And she gradually learned to value her own part in both the relationship and in general.

~~

So do we have to be "perfectly" healthy to have a viable, loving relationship? Fortunately not. In fact, a good relationship can provide the context to work through the residues of our unfinished business from the past. In *Conscious Loving*, the authors, Gay and Kathlyn Hendricks, differentiate between what they call "unconscious loving", where adult intimacy is contaminated by the effects of the past — what we have identified as residual core issue influences — and "conscious loving", where these influences are brought into awareness. This consciousness allows us to work through the remnants of our unfinished business, thus leaving us with the potential to experience more wholehearted and fulfilling connection in our adult relationships.

In *Journey of the Heart,* John Welwood also alludes to a similar concept. He calls this unconscious form of loving "love in the dark", or "sleep", as opposed to being "awake". He sees relationships as an opportunity to expand our sense of who we are, providing we do it with consciousness.

Intimate joining with another person can help us to remove some of the masks developed at earlier times in our life. But it is up to us, not our partner, to effect this change. Welwood believes that the difficulties in our relationships, the buttons that are pushed for us, can be seen as opportunities for growth.

He sees the challenge of relationships as a personal decision: we can choose sleep or wakefulness. If we opt for the safety of sleep, we try to utilise our partner(s) to prop us up and diminish our basic anxiety. We may believe then that it's through the other that we can feel "worthwhile, acceptable, or lovable".

However, a good experience of intimacy, coupled with our own awareness in working through past issues, can help bring unconscious loving to a state of consciousness and enhance our growth and healing. If, however, we continue to love in the dark, we're likely to repeatedly have a lack of satisfaction in a particular relationship, or enter sequential dysfunctional relationships, which have a similar theme, e.g abusive relationships, relationships with a relational or emotionally unavailable partner, submissive relationships where we lose ourselves, etc. These themes stem from our unresolved core issues, which continue to influence our choices and how we relate to our partner(s).

In fact, at an unconscious level, our unfinished business associated with these early childhood residues often influences our choice of partner.

In my first year as a psychology student we were invited to participate in an experiment where a large number of us were in a room with fellow students. We were asked to wander around the room and, without any verbal communication, choose another person. When we were paired, we were asked, again without any verbal communication, to choose another pair.

At this point we were invited to talk about ourselves, our past and our family-of-origin. The links in terms of family order, family dynamics and experiences were remarkable! It is as if an unconscious "invisible thread" had linked us with strangers with similar backgrounds.

This invisible thread is present when we walk into a room of strangers and are attracted or repelled by someone who we don't know at all. And it's the invisible thread that's present when we choose our partners. It's not as random a choice as we might suppose.

We might choose someone who can provide the growing edge for us to work through and resolve some of the unfinished remnants of our past. But this *doesn't* mean expecting the other person to "fix" our problems. We are ultimately responsible for this!

Another person can't fix our insecurity, although a loving, nurturing partner can help us to feel nourished and safe. And in this context the relationship can be a healing relationship: it can provide us with the feeling of being held emotionally, and hence secure enough to embark in our own process of growth. As our buttons are pushed we can come to recognise the residual effects of our core issues and adaptations, and to gradually place them in the past where they originated. Through our own re-parenting process, we can move on into the future.

~~

The recognition of our part *and our power* in the process of healing and re-framing our negative assumptions about ourselves – whether that be individually or within a relationship – allows us to utilise the adult resources within us. These are strengths that were not available to us as children. By being able to reclaim or build those aspects of our real self we had to suppress earlier in our life, we can slowly but surely start to establish strong foundations for a belief that we're okay exactly as we are. We no longer have to constantly try to be something else in order to meet the internal expectations of our Critical Parent or the external demands of others in our world.

The beauty of Inner Child work and the process of re-parenting is that it teaches us that we don't have to be so bound by the constraints of the past, as we move into our mature years. Although there is no absolute point of arrival, we can certainly start to chip away at our old assumptions, our *certainty of misery*, and start to transform our negative self-talk into a more positive acceptance of who we really are.

EXERCISES:

- ***Can you recognise your projections and idealisations in your relationship(s), past or present?***
  - ***Any times when you might have projected your own Critical Parent onto your partner(s)?***
- ***Can you think of ways that through being more "awake" in your relationship(s) you've been able to recognise when your buttons have been pushed? And any times this might have helped you own and work through aspects of your past reflected in adult self-esteem issues?***

- *How comfortable/uncomfortable are you with regards to "boundaries"? Do you take responsibility for "fixing" others, or protecting them in a way that is unhelpful to yourself? Do you find yourself putting your partner(s) first by negating your own needs, and so at a cost to yourself or your own development?*
- *Can you think of ways you might have expected your partner to "fix" your feelings of inadequacy?*
- *What do consider to be your "growing edge", or your greatest challenge in your growth and development with regards to building your self-esteem, whether in a relationship or not?*

Chapter Ten
WHAT NOW?

We've covered the basic "how to" of working towards combating our low self-esteem; and we've looked at our own part in the unhelpful tendency to attack ourselves and hold unrealistic expectations of how we should be. We undermine ourselves through our failure to accept ourselves as intrinsically worthwhile. But we've also seen how, by utilising the Inner Child framework and the concept of re-parenting, we can learn to push back against the destructive Critical Parent part of ourselves. It is through re-parenting that we can start to turn around the damage that has been operating – often unknown to ourselves – and impeding our happiness.

However, it is crucial to recognise that re-parenting is *a process over time*. Understanding what underlies our low self-esteem is the first step, albeit the most important step we can take. But things will not therefore automatically turn around because we now have the understanding. Remember, we need to give our heart time to catch up with our head. And we can't will our psyche to go faster. We can "know" in our head for a long time before we know at that deeper level. But when that transformation takes place the feeling is quite different.

If we can hold the awareness of the framework we've been exploring, and keep working on that internal relationship between the residual child parts and our more mature adult resources, the old internal dictates can *gradually* transform to newer, more constructive attitudes towards ourselves. And we now have a knowledge foundation as a base. If we're mindful but patient with ourselves we can, little by little, start to challenge our old assumptions. As soon as we start to register that we're feeling bad about ourselves, this is a signal to us that our Nurturing and Protective Parent parts have gone to sleep.

It's helpful to keep returning to the work. We can utilise the re-parenting methods set out in Chapter Three, where we dialogue with our Inner Child, either through the written dialogues, the empty chair or meditation. We can keep asking our Inner Child how she/he is feeling, and what they're needing from us. We can become more mindful of that critical voice within that batters our Inner Child. It might be useful to revisit the exercises at the end of each chapter from time to time. And it's also important to become more mindful of our *shoulds* and our *shouldn'ts* (the language of our Critical Parent), and instead check in with what we *want* or *need* (the language of our Nurturing Parent).

We also need to continue to remind ourselves that we're okay *just because we're who we are*. This will not come easily initially, because the status quo - our familiar *certainty of misery* - is likely to draw us back like a magnet. Old habits do indeed die hard.

Our Critical Parent doesn't disappear. But through becoming more aware and exercising our constructive adult nurturing and protective resources we can start to make these attributes more familiar and therefore more automatic over time. We'll gradually spend less time in collusion with our Critical Parent, and our visits to this destructive realm become less intense.

Sometimes during this process it's helpful to tune into our posture. When we're feeling depleted of confidence we tend to curl up, make ourselves smaller, usually without realising we're doing this. We're identifying with our Vulnerable Inner Child, and this emotional feeling is being expressed through our body. It's useful to try sitting or standing taller, by dropping our shoulders, straightening our spine and lifting our head towards the ceiling or sky. It's surprising how this small action can be beneficial: our body can symbolically remind our psyche that we also have our adult self to rely on.

The process of change is a little like learning to drive a car: initially we focus on all the components of the driving lesson. It might feel overwhelming at first, as we try to juggle new information about road rules, braking, turning the wheel, the clutch, etc. But gradually, over time and with practice, driving becomes more natural. So, too, our re-parenting process can become more automatic.

Importantly, we need to take care not to let our Critical Parent become impatient as we embark on this journey; we must beware not to deride ourselves for being unable to immediately turn things around. Remember, it's not a test or a race.

~~

You've probably read this book because you're wanting to change something that has been destructive or painful. But you've had years of relating to yourself in a particular way, years of telling yourself that you do not measure up. And whilst it doesn't have to take the same amount of time to change this old pattern, neither will it happen overnight. You have the tools to assist you in this important journey towards a more comfortable relationship with yourself, a relationship involving caring and protecting yourself from the barbs of your internal critic.

I often use the metaphor of a mountain: when we have a goal or task, we tend to look at the top of the mountain. And this can make us feel hopeless. We tell ourselves it's too high, too steep, too far and it will take us forever – *if* we can ever make it at all. We need to take our gaze away from the top of the mountain, and just be aware of the next step. And then the next step. And at some stage, if we focus on small manageable portions – just one step at a time – we may surprise ourselves if we glance down and see we've actually come further up the mountain than we realised! So be gentle with yourself and trust your own process.

BIBLIOGRAPHY

BRADSHAW, JOHN.　　　*Homecoming*　(New York: Bantam, 1990)

CAPACCHIONE, LUCIA　　*Recovery of Your Inner Child*　(New York: Simon & Schuster/Fireside, 1991)

ERIKSON, ERIK H.　　　*Childhood and Society*　(New York: W.W. Norton & Co., 1993)

HENDRICKS, GAY and
HENDRICKS, KATHLYN　*Conscious Loving*　(U.S.A: Bantam Doubleday Dell Publishing Group Inc., 1980)

HORNEY, KAREN　　　*Neurosis and Human Growth*　(U.K: Routledge, 2013)

KINGMA, DAPHNE ROSE　*Finding True Love*　(CA: Conari Press, 2001)

WELWOOD, JOHN　　　*Journey of the Heart*　(New York: Harper Collins, 1996)

www.ingramcontent.com/pod-product-compliance
Lightning Source LLC
LaVergne TN
LVHW051848080426
835512LV00018B/3135